Algorithms
with
Disney
FROZEN

Allyssa Loya

Lerner Publications ◆ Minneapolis

005.1

Lerner Publications Company
A division of Lerner Publishing Group, Inc.
241 First Avenue North
Minneapolis, MN 55401 USA

For reading levels and more information, look up this title at www.lernerbooks.com.

Additional graphics provided by Laura Westlund/Independent Picture Service.

Main body text set in Billy Infant Regular 14/20.
Typeface provided by SparkyType.

Library of Congress Cataloging-in-Publication Data

Names: Loya, Allyssa, author.
Title: Algorithms with Frozen / Allyssa Loya.
Description: Minneapolis : Lerner Publications, [2018] | Series: Disney coding adventures | Includes bibliographical references and index. | Audience: Ages 6-9. | Audience: Grades K to 3.
Identifiers: LCCN 2017061823 (print) | LCCN 2017061477 (ebook) | ISBN 9781541524323 (eb pdf) | ISBN 9781541524286 (lb : alk. paper) | ISBN 9781541526754 (pb : alk. paper)
Subjects: LCSH: Computer algorithms—Juvenile literature. | Frozen (Motion picture : 2013)—Juvenile literature.
Classification: LCC QA76.9.A43 (print) | LCC QA76.9.A43 L675 2018 (ebook) | DDC 005.1—dc23

LC record available at https://lccn.loc.gov/2017061823

Manufactured in the United States of America
1-44516-34766-2/28/2018

Bc# 000004371

Table of Contents

What Is an Algorithm?

How do computers know what to do? Do they have brains? No! That's silly. A person writes lines of code that tell a computer what to do. *Algorithm* is a big word for something easy. It is a group of instructions that tells your computer how to solve a problem or finish a job. A lot of code put together makes up an algorithm.

When you're walking, for example, think of one step as a line of code. To get outside, you might need an algorithm that starts with ten steps. Next, you open the door, and finally, you step outside.

You can use algorithms to help your favorite *Frozen* characters solve problems. For some of these activities, you'll need a partner, plain paper, construction paper, scissors, pencils, and crayons.

Do You Want to Draw a Snowman?

Anna wants to build a snowman. It's one of her favorite things to do with Elsa. The sisters love working on the snowman together.

What if you wanted to draw the same snowman as a friend did, but you didn't know what steps to take? That's a great way to practice algorithms with a partner! First, grab some paper, pencils, and something to hide your drawing.

Next, draw a snowman. Don't let your partner see it! Then decompose it. That means think about the steps you took to draw it. You'll tell your partner each step to take to draw the same snowman. Be as specific as you can.

When you're done, share your drawings. Are they the same?

When you write an algorithm, you need to be specific so the computer understands your instructions.

Get to Troll Valley!

Anna needs help. Her family needs to get her to Troll Valley as soon as possible!

First, look at the grid on this page. Think about how someone would get from the starting point to Grand Pabbie without hitting anything. Use your finger to count the squares in each direction. Then look at the lines of arrows in the answer choices. Each arrow gives an instruction. Together, the arrows make up a line of code.

Which line of code would get someone from the starting square to Grand Pabbie?

A ↓ ↓ ↓ → → →

B → → ↓ ↓ → ↓

C ↓ → → → ↓ ↓

Try this one next. How would you get from the starting square to Grand Pabbie?

A ➡️⬇️⬇️⬇️➡️➡️

B ➡️➡️➡️⬇️⬇️⬇️

C ⬇️⬇️➡️➡️⬇️⬇️

START

If Anna's parents were in the starting square, how would they get to Grand Pabbie?

A ➡️➡️➡️

B ➡️➡️➡️⬇️⬇️⬇️

C ➡️⬇️⬇️⬇️

Check your answers on page 30.

Saving Anna

Grand Pabbie needs help finding
Anna's memories!

In this activity, you'll write an algorithm to help Grand Pabbie get to Anna's memories. Look at the grid, and decompose the challenge.

On your own paper, draw arrows that will move the wise troll from the starting square to Anna's memories. Watch out for trees and rocks! Think of each arrow as one step of instruction. All the arrows together will make up the algorithm.

Meant-to-Be Handshake

Prince Hans and Anna think they are meant to be together and can finish each other's . . . sandwiches!

Grab a partner, and create a meant-to-be handshake. Each handshake drawing is like one line of code. To make a meant-to-be handshake, you will put the handshake parts together into an algorithm.

First, think through how you want your handshake to look. Use steps from the pictures, or make up your own. Then, on a separate sheet of paper, draw the steps in order. Finally, you and your partner will run, or start, the algorithm and complete the handshake!

Building an Ice Castle

Elsa is on the North Mountain, building the ice castle of her dreams.

If you were building a castle, you might repeat some steps. If you needed to do the same thing many times in your code, you might use a loop. Loops tell computers how many times to do the same thing. That can make writing code go faster.

Both of these algorithms mean to move to the right five times.

$$5(\rightarrow) = \rightarrow \rightarrow \rightarrow \rightarrow \rightarrow$$

The first one is a loop. It tells us how many times to repeat the same move. Writing the loop is faster than writing out each step.

The main parts of this castle are ready to be put together. Look at the castle pieces, and pick the algorithm that moves each piece to where it should go. Which loop moves wall 1 into place?

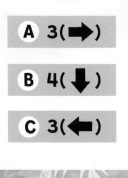

A 3(➡)

B 4(⬇)

C 3(⬅)

wall 1

floor

ceiling

wall 1

wall 2

floor

Which loop moves the ceiling into place? Which loop moves wall 2 to where it needs to go?

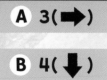

A 3(➡)

B 4(⬇)

C 3(⬅)

Sven Needs to Eat

Sven is so hungry! He can hardly wait to have a snack.

Look at the grid. You can use loops to create the easiest way for Sven to get to every single carrot. Sven is your starting point. Write loops with arrows, such as 5(➡), on your own paper to create your algorithm.

Escaping the Giant Snowman

Anna, Kristoff, and Olaf are racing away from Elsa's giant snowman. Make them a clear path to follow.

First, draw a grid of at least four rows and four columns on a sheet of paper. Next, add a starting square, an ending square, and trees, rocks, and rivers to some of the squares. Make sure your grid has at least one clear path out.

Then give your grid to a partner. Ask your partner to use arrows and loops to write an algorithm that will get the friends to safety.

Troll Celebration

Kristoff's family of trolls loves to sing and dance.

You and a partner can use algorithms to make up your own dance. When you make up a dance, think about what moves to include. For example, steps might be jump, hands up, touch the floor, and stand up.

Be sure to include all the steps of your dance in order. Use loops if you like! Write the steps down if you need to. Then boogie! When you follow these dance moves, it's as if you are the computer following an algorithm. Have fun!

Let's Go!

Anna's heart is freezing. She needs to get back to Arendelle Castle.

In this project, you will make a path to help Anna get back home. Your partner will write the algorithm. Draw a 6 by 4 grid on a sheet of construction paper. See the grid on the next page for an example. Your grid should fill the whole sheet of paper. Next, cut on the grid's lines to make 24 squares.

Line up your construction paper squares to create a twisty, turning path that will get Anna back home. Look at the example. Use as many squares as you want for your path.

Your partner will decompose the problem. Then, using a clean sheet of paper, your partner will draw arrows to write an algorithm to guide Anna down the mountain. Don't forget about loops!

Run, or begin, the algorithm. If you come across any bugs, or mistakes, in the code, fix them and run the algorithm again.

Make this activity more exciting! Use your squares to make a different path. Add challenges by putting in new squares. Or include trees, logs, or other objects to go around.

In Summer

When it gets hot, Olaf starts to melt. Thankfully, he has Elsa's magic cloud to help him stay frozen. But if that cloud disappears, he'll be a puddle!

Code works great if it's written perfectly. But if there's a bug, a computer can't follow the directions. Look at Olaf's path in the lines of code on the next page. If there's a sun above his path, he needs his cloud. If there is no sun, he can just keep walking. If you don't see a cloud below a sun, that's a bug.

Look through the code to find the bugs. How would you rewrite the lines of code to resolve, or fix, the bugs?

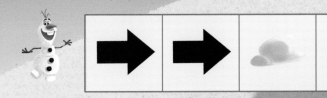

Keep Coding!

Now that you know that algorithms are just sets of clear instructions, you can find lots of chances to practice your coding skills. As you go about your day, think about the steps you are taking. How would you clearly explain them to someone else?

When you make something to eat, do you use a spoon or a fork? Do you need to grab it, then pick it up, and then stir? When you get dressed, which piece of clothing is first? Which arm or leg is first?

When you go ice skating, where do you need to put your feet? Which foot moves first? Do you move forward or backward?

Breaking down tasks in this way helps you think like a coder. What other activities can you write algorithms for?

Answer Key

Page 8–9: 1. A; 2. B; 3. C

Page 11 (possible answers):

⬇➡➡⬇⬇⬇➡➡ or ⬇⬇⬇➡➡➡⬇➡➡

Pages 14–15: wall 1 = A; ceiling = B; wall 2 = C

Page 17 (possible answer):

⬇➡ 3(⬆) 3(➡) 2(⬆) 5(⬅)

Page 27:

❄➡➡❄❄➡➡, ❄➡❄❄➡❄❄, ➡❄❄❄➡❄➡

Glossary

algorithm: a group of instructions, made up of lines of code, that tell your computer how to solve a problem or finish a job

bug: a mistake found in lines of code

code: instructions for computers that are written in a way that computers can follow

decompose: to take a big problem and break it down into small pieces to figure it out

loop: a line of code that tells the computer to repeat an instruction a certain number of times

resolve: to fix a mistake (a bug) in lines of code

run: to start a program

Further Information

CodeMonkey
https://www.playcodemonkey.com

Code.org
https://code.org/learn

Lyons, Heather, and Elizabeth Tweedale. *Learn to Program*. Minneapolis: Lerner Publications, 2017.

Matteson, Adrienne. *Coding with ScratchJr*. Ann Arbor, MI: Cherry Lake, 2017.

Prottsman, Kiki. *My First Coding Book*. New York: DK, 2017.

Index

About the Author

Allyssa Loya is an elementary school librarian in North Texas. Her passion for bringing meaningful learning to students led her to cultivate a technology-forward library that includes a makerspace and a coding club. While running the coding club in the library, she realized how important it is for every student to experience coding. Not every student will grow up to be a computer programmer, but all students will need to know how to think clearly and critically when they are adults.

Loya is married to an IT manager, who is a perfect support system for her technological endeavors. Her two young boys are a constant reminder of the experiences that all students deserve from their educators.